I CAN BE A
TRUCK DRIVER

By June Behrens

Prepared under the direction of Robert Hillerich, Ph.D.

CHILDRENS PRESS™

CHICAGO

Library of Congress Cataloging in Publication Data
Behrens, June.
    I can be a truck driver.

    Summary: Describes in simple terms the training and
duties of a truck driver.
    Includes index.
    1. Truck driving—Vocational guidance—Juvenile
literature. [1. Truck driving—Vocational guidance.
2. Occupations] I. Title. II. Title: Truck driver.
HD8039.M795B44 1985   388.3'24'02373   84-23246
ISBN 0-516-01848-5

PICTURE DICTIONARY

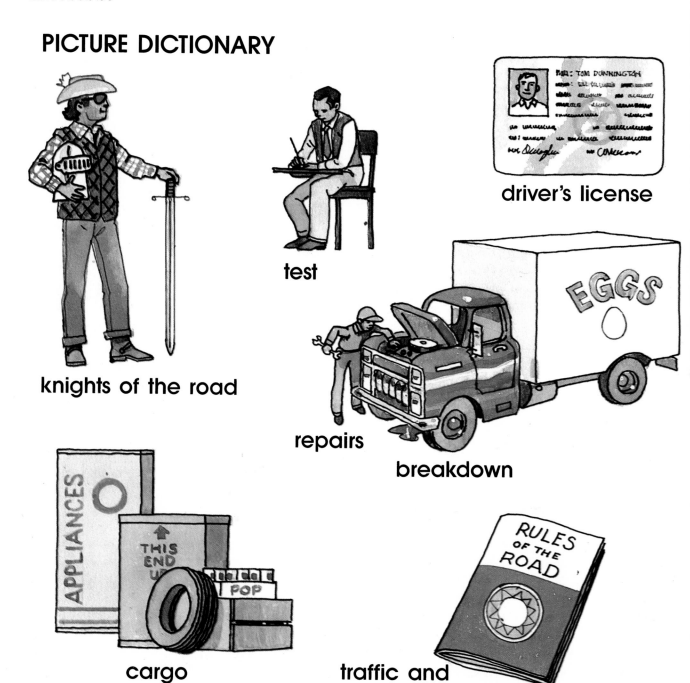

driver's license

test

knights of the road

repairs

breakdown

cargo

traffic and
safety rules

deliveries   **one-piece truck**
(one-piece truck on one frame)

logbook   **records**

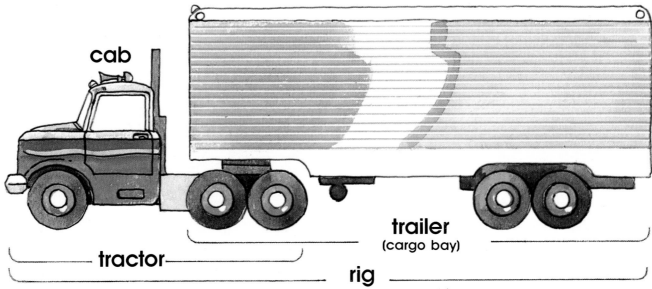

cab

tractor

trailer
(cargo bay)

rig
(tractor and trailer truck)

state lines

roadeo

Truck driver climbs into the cab of his truck.

Trucks carry the things
we eat, wear, and use.
Truck drivers are called
"knights of the road."

knights of the road

Have you watched big
trucks go by?

Would you like to be a
truck driver?

test

driver's license

Truck drivers must be
healthy and strong. They
must pass a test and
have a driver's license.
They must be good
drivers.

Truck drivers go to
school. They learn all
about traffic and safety
rules. They must know
about the cargo their
trucks carry. Cargo is
anything that can be
moved. They learn to
load and unload big

traffic and safety rules

cargo

Driver writes
in his logbook.

logbook

records

trucks. They keep
logbooks. Logbooks are
written records of
everything that happens
on a trucker's trip.

Delivery truck (left) and tow truck (right) are one-piece trucks.

Student truck drivers, or truckers, learn to drive all kinds of trucks. A one-piece truck has the engine, cab, and cargo space on one frame.

one-piece truck
(one-piece truck on one frame)

Tanker truck (left) and refrigerator truck (right) have two parts.

tractor — trailer
rig
(tractor and trailer truck)

Tractor and trailer
trucks are called rigs.
They are in two or more
parts. The tractor is the
truck body, with the
engine and cab. The
trailer carries the cargo. It
is hitched to the tractor.

Student driver learns how to back up a tractor to a trailer.

Student drivers learn to
pull short trailers and
long trailers.

Students learn about truck engines.

Trucker fixes a fuel leak.

Student drivers must know about the trucks they drive. They learn to make simple repairs if there is a breakdown.

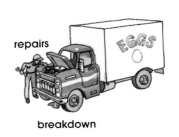

repairs

breakdown

deliveries

Some truck drivers work
in and around cities.
They move cargo on
short trips. They pick up
and deliver goods. These
truckers often stop to

Driver records the amount of goods he picked up for delivery.

load and unload their cargo. Drivers keep records of deliveries and sometimes collect money.

Dump truck

Moving truck

Garbage truck

Milk truck

Truckers drive milk
trucks and bakery trucks
in cities and towns. They
drive delivery trucks and
mail trucks. They drive
moving vans and dump
trucks. They bring food
to stores and take trash
away from homes.

These drivers can back
their big trucks into tight
places. They drive safely
on narrow and crowded
city streets. These truckers
usually go home at night.

Other truckers are long-
distance drivers. They
may be away from home
for days. They sit behind
the wheels of their trucks
most of the time. Drivers
may carry their cargo

thousands of miles. Long-distance truckers drive from city to city. They cross state lines. They must know about driving rules in different states.

state lines

Drivers must know about their cargo. They must know how much their truck weighs, too. It is against the law to carry cargo that weighs too much on highways.

Driver checks the hoses on her truck.

Before a trip, drivers
look over their trucks.
They make sure the
cargo is loaded right. On
a trip they write about
the truck, the roads, and
the cargo. Everything is
written in the logbook.

23

At truck stops, drivers can get fuel, buy spare parts, eat food, and talk to their fellow truckers.

Long-distance truckers are called over-the-road drivers. Sometimes they are called long-haul drivers. They work on a time schedule. They drive long distances every day.

Sleeper berth
in a truck

They stop only when
they have to eat or sleep.
Many long-distance
truckers even sleep in
their trucks.

Roadeo driver takes tight turn without touching side rails.

roadeo

Have you heard of a roadeo? A roadeo is a contest to find the best truck driver. The driver must know everything about trucks and driving them. Truckers come from

everywhere to drive in a
roadeo. The best driver is
the roadeo champion.

Truck drivers know
about speed limits. They
know about the weather
and roads. They know

about their big trucks
and how to move their
cargo. Truck drivers say,
"If you've got it. . .a truck
brought it."

Would you like to be a
truck driver?

WORDS YOU SHOULD KNOW

breakdown (BRAIK • down)—a failure to work, sometimes through breaking

cab (KAB)—the part of a truck where the driver sits to operate the controls

cargo (KAR • goh)—anything that can be moved by a truck

champion (CHAM • pee • un)—the winner of a contest

delivery (di • LIV • er • ee)—the act of moving something from one place to another

driver's license (DRYVE • erz LY • sens)—a permit that allows a person to drive a car; it is issued by a governmental office

goods (GOODS)—cargo; things carried on a truck

healthy (HELTH • ee)—having good health

knights (NYTS)—in olden times, brave men who fought on horseback

logbooks (LOG • books)—written records of things that happen on a trip

long-distance (LONG-DIS • tents)—over a lengthy route

over-the-road drivers (OH • ver THUH ROAD DRYVE • erz)—long-distance truckers, also known as long-haul drivers

rigs (RIGS)—a name for tractor and trailer trucks

roadeo (ROAD • ee • oh)—a truck-driving contest to find the best driver

rules (ROOLS)—laws or regulations that must be obeyed

safety (SAYF • tee)—being safe from getting hurt or injured

tractor (TRAK • ter)—a truck body, with engine and cab

traffic (TRAF • ik)—the movement of cars, trucks, and other vehicles

trailer (TRAY • ler)—the part of a truck hitched to the tractor; it carries the cargo

trucker (TRUHK • er)—a truck driver

INDEX

PHOTO CREDITS
Courtesy American Trucking Associations, Inc.—22 (bottom), 23
Courtesy Associates Commercial Corporation—4, 10 (left), 28 (bottom left)
© Reinhard Brucker—5, 9 (right), 10 (right), 16 (bottom), 17 (right)
© Jacqueline Durand—14 (left)
EKM-Nepenthe:
    © Robert V. Eckert Jr.—20, 22 (top)
Courtesy Heavy Duty Trucking Magazine—Cover
Courtesy International Harvester—9 (left), 16 (top), 21 (two photos), 25, 29
Courtesy Jewel Food Stores—7
Courtesy Mack Trucks, Inc.—14 (right)
Courtesy MTA Inc.—11, 12, 13, 17 (left), 19, 26
Nawrocki Stock Photo:
    © Joseph Jacobson—28 (top)
    © W. S. Nawrocki—24 (right)
    © Ken Sexton—18
    ©Jim Wright—27 (left), 28 (right)
©Art Pahlke—8, 15
Reprinted with permission from Road King Magazine—6, 27 (right)
Courtesy Marathon Oil Co.—24 (left)

About the Author

JUNE BEHRENS has written more than fifty books, plays, and filmstrips for young people, touching on all subject areas of the school curriculum. Mrs. Behrens has for many years been an educator in one of California's largest public school systems. She is a graduate of the University of California at Santa Barbara and has a Master's degree from the University of Southern California. Mrs. Behrens is listed in *Who's Who of American Women*. She is a recipient of the Distinguished Alumni Award from the University of California for her contributions in the field of education. She and her husband live in Rancho Palos Verdes, a southern California suburb.